# WHAT IS IT, TINK, IS PAN IN TROUBLE?

# Doonesbury Books by G.B. Trudeau

## In Large Format

# A DOONESBURY BOOK
## by G. B. TRUDEAU

# WHAT IS IT, TINK, IS PAN IN TROUBLE?

ANDREWS and McMEEL     A UNIVERSAL PRESS SYNDICATE COMPANY     KANSAS CITY

——————————— ATTENTION: SCHOOLS AND BUSINESSES ———————————

Andrews and McMeel books are available at quantity discounts with bulk purchase for educational, business, or sales promotional use. For information, please write to: Special Sales Department, Andrews and McMeel, 4900 Main Street, Kansas City, Missouri 64112.

"There's a non-partisan — no, but I really mean this one, that from the heart in the sense that some things, at least the way I look at this."

— PRESIDENT GEORGE BUSH,
campaigning in New Hampshire

6

8

9

11

12

THE THING OF IT IS, RAY, YOU NEVER WANT TO RULE OUT THE POSSIBILITY THAT YOUR OLD LADY MIGHT COME TO HER SENSES.

I MEAN, LOOK AT MY SITUATION. WHEN I FIRST MET MEG ON THE LOVE BOAT, I THOUGHT SHE WAS IT! DONE DEAL! I WAS ALL SET TO CUT BOOPSIE LOOSE...

THEN THE THING WENT SOUR, AND IT HIT ME HOW CLOSE I CAME TO BLOWING THE BEST THING I EVER HAD! SO, AS FAR AS I'M CONCERNED, MEG NEVER HAPPENED! SHE DOESN'T EVEN EXIST!

... AND SO I DECIDED TO COME BACK AND FIGHT FOR HIM!

WHO **ARE** YOU?

DO YOU EXPECT HIM BACK SOON? I KNOW I SHOULD HAVE CALLED AHEAD, BUT I WAS AFRAID HE WOULDN'T SPEAK TO ME.

LET ME GET THIS STRAIGHT. YOU'RE A FORMER "FRIEND" OF B.D.'S, AND YOU'VE SHOWN UP HERE UNANNOUNCED HOPING TO PICK UP WHERE YOU LEFT OFF?

WELL, YEAH. IF I'M NOT TOO LATE.

AND YOU'RE WHAT, HIS CLEANING LADY?

FILLED YOU RIGHT IN, DID HE?

IT REALLY WAS PERFECT. I MEAN, IT WAS A ROMANTIC SETTING, AND NEITHER OF US HAD ANYONE WAITING AT HOME. THE ONLY PROBLEM WAS THAT HE WASN'T AN OFFICER LIKE ME, AND THE ARMY HAS RULES ABOUT THAT...

HEY, I'M NOT BORING YOU WITH MY LITTLE ROMANTIC PROBLEMS, AM I?

NOT AT ALL. I'M ANXIOUS TO HEAR THE FULL STORY.

YOU'RE NICE. BY THE WAY, THE HOUSE LOOKS ABSOLUTELY IMMACULATE.

EXCUSE ME?

UM... YOU **ARE** HIS CLEANING LADY, AREN'T YOU?

AS I LOOK BACK ON IT NOW, YES.

13

16

HEY, *GENTLE READER!* CONFOUNDED BY THE PROLIFERATION OF CHARACTERS AND RELATIONSHIPS IN THIS FEATURE? AREN'T MOST 19TH CENTURY RUSSIAN NOVELS MORE COMPREHENSIBLE?

DON'T DESPAIR! LIKE MOST BIG-TIME OPERATIONS, DOONESBURY HAS AN EASY-TO-FOLLOW ORGANIZATIONAL CHART! AND NOW, FOR THE FIRST TIME, IT'S BEING MADE AVAILABLE TO YOU AT THE LOW, LOW COST OF THIS SUNDAY PAPER! *ENJOY!*

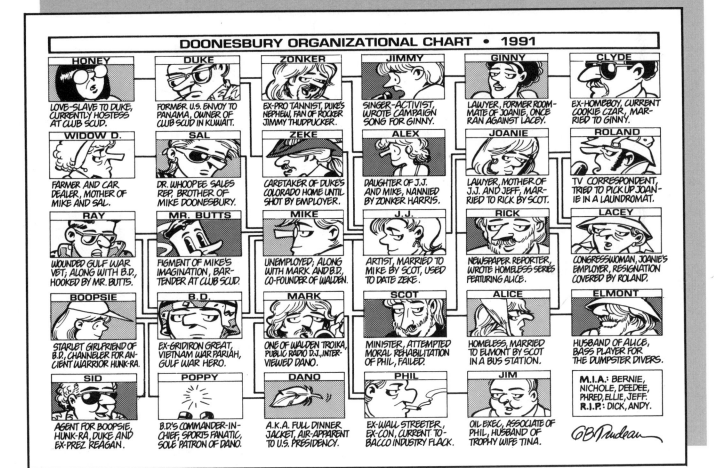

## DOONESBURY ORGANIZATIONAL CHART • 1991

**HONEY** — LOVE-SLAVE TO DUKE, CURRENTLY HOSTESS AT CLUB SCUD.

**DUKE** — FORMER U.S. ENVOY TO PANAMA, OWNER OF CLUB SCUD IN KUWAIT.

**ZONKER** — EX-PRO TANNIST, DUKE'S NEPHEW, FAN OF ROCKER JIMMY THUDPUCKER.

**JIMMY** — SINGER-ACTIVIST, WROTE CAMPAIGN SONG FOR GINNY.

**GINNY** — LAWYER, FORMER ROOMMATE OF JOANIE, ONCE RAN AGAINST LACEY.

**CLYDE** — EX-HOMEBOY, CURRENT COOKIE CZAR, MARRIED TO GINNY.

**WIDOW D.** — FARMER AND CAR DEALER, MOTHER OF MIKE AND SAL.

**SAL** — DR. WHOOPEE SALES REP, BROTHER OF MIKE DOONESBURY.

**ZEKE** — CARETAKER OF DUKE'S COLORADO HOME UNTIL SHOT BY EMPLOYER.

**ALEX** — DAUGHTER OF J.J. AND MIKE, NANNIED BY ZONKER HARRIS.

**JOANIE** — LAWYER, MOTHER OF J.J. AND JEFF, MARRIED TO RICK BY SCOT.

**ROLAND** — TV CORRESPONDENT, TRIED TO PICK UP JOANIE IN A LAUNDROMAT.

**RAY** — WOUNDED GULF WAR VET; ALONG WITH B.D., HOOKED BY MR. BUTTS.

**MR. BUTTS** — FIGMENT OF MIKE'S IMAGINATION, BARTENDER AT CLUB SCUD.

**MIKE** — UNEMPLOYED; ALONG WITH MARK AND B.D., CO-FOUNDER OF WALDEN.

**J.J.** — ARTIST, MARRIED TO MIKE BY SCOT, USED TO DATE ZEKE.

**RICK** — NEWSPAPER REPORTER, WROTE HOMELESS SERIES FEATURING ALICE.

**LACEY** — CONGRESSWOMAN, JOANIE'S EMPLOYER, RESIGNATION COVERED BY ROLAND.

**BOOPSIE** — STARLET GIRLFRIEND OF B.D., CHANNELER FOR ANCIENT WARRIOR HUNK-RA.

**B.D.** — EX-GRIDIRON GREAT, VIETNAM WAR PARIAH, GULF WAR HERO.

**MARK** — ONE OF WALDEN TROIKA, PUBLIC RADIO D.J., INTERVIEWED DANO.

**SCOT** — MINISTER, ATTEMPTED MORAL REHABILITATION OF PHIL, FAILED.

**ALICE** — HOMELESS, MARRIED TO ELMONT BY SCOT IN A BUS STATION.

**ELMONT** — HUSBAND OF ALICE, BASS PLAYER FOR THE DUMPSTER DIVERS.

**SID** — AGENT FOR BOOPSIE, HUNK-RA, DUKE AND EX-PREZ REAGAN.

**POPPY** — B.D.'S COMMANDER-IN-CHIEF, SPORTS FANATIC, SOLE PATRON OF DANO.

**DANO** — A.K.A. FULL DINNER JACKET, AIR-APPARENT TO U.S. PRESIDENCY.

**PHIL** — EX-WALL STREETER, EX-CON, CURRENT TOBACCO INDUSTRY FLACK.

**JIM** — OIL EXEC, ASSOCIATE OF PHIL, HUSBAND OF TROPHY WIFE TINA.

**M.I.A.:** BERNIE, NICHOLE, DEEDEE, PHRED, ELLIE, JEFF. **R.I.P.:** DICK, ANDY.

GBTrudeau

B.D.!

HI YA, BUDDY. HOPE I'M NOT INTERRUPTING ANYTHING...

NO, I...

GOOD, BECAUSE I'M IN A JAM. BOOPSIE GAVE ME THE BOOT. CAN YOU BELIEVE THAT?

I'VE BEEN DRIVING FOR THREE DAYS STRAIGHT, AND I REALLY NEED A PLACE TO CRASH AND SORT OUT MY LIFE! YOU DON'T MIND, DO YOU?

WELL, AS A MATTER OF FACT...

ME, TOO.

B.D., I'M SORRY ABOUT YOU AND BOOPSIE, BUT YOU AND YOUR FRIEND CAN'T STAY HERE NOW...

MIKE, IT'D JUST BE FOR A WEEK OR SO...

B.D., IT'S NOT A GOOD TIME FOR A VISIT. YOU'LL JUST HAVE TO TRUST ME ON THIS...

HEY, C'MON, HOW BAD CAN THINGS BE? WE JUST WANT TO CRASH IN YOUR LIVING ROOM FOR A WHILE. NICE COUCHES, BY THE WAY...

THANK YOU. THIS FALL, WE'LL BE BURNING THEM FOR HEAT.

YO, LET'S GO, MAN. THIS PLACE IS A DUMP.

I'M SORRY, B.D., BUT I JUST CAN'T PUT YOU UP NOW...

HEY, C'MON MIKE— I'M HURTIN' HERE.

EVEN IF I COULD PERSUADE BOOPSIE TO TAKE ME BACK, SHE'S NOT GETTING JOBS, WHICH MEANS THAT AS HER MANAGER, I DON'T HAVE A JOB...

YEAH, WELL, I'M OUT OF WORK MYSELF. AND J.J.'S NOT SELLING ANY OF HER STUFF. AND ZONKER, OF COURSE, HASN'T HELD A REAL JOB IN HIS LIFE!

AREN'T WE JUST A CREDIT TO OUR ALMA MATER?

YOU PEOPLE WENT TO COLLEGE?

24

25

26

# Duke's world

THE PUTSCH OF THE SUPPORTING CHARACTERS, CONT'D.

...AND SINCE THE GANG OF EIGHT REPLACED THE BIG THREE, RATINGS FOR THE ONCE-BELOVED SUNDAY FEATURE HAVE PLUMMETED!

WHY IS HE STILL IN THE STRIP? HE MUST BE REMOVED AT ONCE!

I TOLD YOU WE HAD TO GET THE MEDIA ON OUR SIDE!

IT WOULDN'T HAVE MATTERED. THE COUP WAS DOOMED FROM THE START!

SO WHY'D YOU SIGN ON THEN, THEN, MR. S-S-SECOND THOUGHTS?

HE DIDN'T! HE'S A PASSIVE CHARACTER! I TOLD YOU HE WASN'T ON BOARD! DOES ANYBODY LISTEN TO ME? NOOO!

THIS IS NOT WORKING OUT, GUYS. JUST LOOK AT US! WE'RE EVEN LOSING COLOR INTENSITY!

IT'S THE PRESIDENT'S FAULT! HE'S SUPPOSED TO HANDLE THESE THINGS! THE FEATURE'S GOT HIS NAME ON IT, FOR CRYING OUT LOUD!

MR. PRESIDENT? MR. PRESIDENT? LOOKS LIKE WE'VE LOST HIM...

HOT DAMN! I'M NEXT IN SUCCESSION!

SLAP! SLAP! SLAP!

THEY WANT YOU BACK.

I'LL THINK ABOUT IT.

**THE COUP, CONCLUDED.**

HI. SINCE THE RECENT BOTCHED COUP OF THE SUPPORTING CHARACTERS, SOME OF YOU HAVE BEEN MAKING INQUIRIES ABOUT THE WELFARE OF THE EIGHT RINGLEADERS.

DON'T WORRY, THE OPPORTUNING LITTLE WEASELS ARE ALL HEALTHY, ALTHOUGH THAT WASN'T **MY** IDEA. FOR INDIVIDUAL OUTCOMES, CHECK THE CONSPIRATOR RAP SHEETS BELOW.

**THE PLOTTERS**

**AMBASSADOR DUKE:**
SUSPENDED FROM DAILY STRIP FOR SIX WEEKS. BANNED FROM COLOR SUNDAY COMICS UNTIL 1993. INELIGIBLE FOR INDUCTION INTO COMICS HALL OF FAME.

**PHIL SLACKMEYER:**
PERMANENTLY BANNED FROM SUNDAY COMICS. STRIPPED OF SECURITY CLEARANCE. MUST WEAR ELECTRONIC BRACELET WHEN APPEARING IN DAILY FEATURE.

**R-R-RON HEADREST:**
BANISHED FOR FIVE SEASONS TO LOCAL-ACCESS CABLE, WITH NO CHANCE OF RENEWAL. MAY NOT APPEAR ON ANY VIDEO SCREEN LARGER THAN 9".

**JIM ANDREWS:**
STRIPPED OF STANDING IN NATIONAL SATIRE RANKINGS BY COMMISSIONER OF COMICS. ELIGIBLE FOR WALK-ON ROLES IN SPRING OF 1997.

**ZEKE BRENNER:**
ORDERED TO SPEND THREE MONTHS IN A HALF-WAY STRIP, "ZIPPY THE PINHEAD." SENTENCE SUSPENDED IN EXCHANGE FOR FINGERING OTHER PLOTTERS.

**SAL DOONESBURY:**
ALONG WITH DANO, BECAME "ILL" WHEN PLOT STARTED TO UNRAVEL. HAS SINCE DISAPPEARED; THOUGHT TO BE WORKING IN UNDERGROUND COMIX.

**VICE PRESIDENT DANO:**
PLED "YOUTHFUL INDISCRETION"; BANNED FROM PLAYING GOLF DURING OFFICE HOURS. TRADED TO DISNEY FOR A CHARACTER TO BE NAMED, PLUS CASH.

**ZONKER HARRIS:**
ENTERED PLEA OF INNOCENT, CLAIMING HE THOUGHT COUP MEMBERS WERE PLANNING SURPRISE BIRTHDAY PARTY FOR MIKE. CASE DISMISSED; DEFENDANT RETURNED TO PARENTS.

GBTrudeau

33

34

36

OH, NO... HERE COMES WOODY.

WHO'S WOODY?

A JERK I USED TO KNOW AT LAW SCHOOL. HE'S G.O.P. COUNSEL FOR SENATE JUDICIARY.

OH, SURE, I'VE HEARD OF THIS GUY...

SUZANNE, NO! DON'T MAKE EYE CONTACT!

HI, GIRLS! I'M TRYING TO "GET IT"! WANT TO HELP ME "GET IT"?

SORRY.

THOUGHT YOU'D JUST PULL UP A CHAIR AND GLOAT, EH, WOODY?

HEE, HEE! NO, BUT COULD YOU BLAME ME? LOOKS LIKE OUR SIDE IS GOING TO GET QUITE A GOOD HIT OFF THE THOMAS HEARINGS!

LOVE TO HEAR WHY, BUT I'M LATE TO A MEETING...

WHAT?

UH-OH! CLEAR SIGNALS CITY! HA, HA!

OH, WELL! I REALLY PREFER TALKING TO YOU ONE-ON-ONE ANYWAY, JOAN GIRL!

WHY WOULD THAT BE, WOOD BOY?

NO WITNESSES! HA, HA, HA! JUST KIDDING! GET YOU A COKE? HA, HA, HA! JOKE! JOKE!

WOODY, I'VE ALWAYS FOUND YOU OFFENSIVE, BUT I HAVE TO SAY, YOU'VE JUST TOPPED...

JOANIE, JOANIE, LIGHTEN UP!

I'M JUST KIDDING! I'M A KIDDER, YOU KNOW THAT! AND KIDDING ASIDE, THE LAST FEW WEEKS I HAVE LEARNED A LOT ABOUT WOMEN AND THEIR CONCERNS!

IT'S BEEN AN EDUCATION. ON SOME LEVEL, I'LL PROBABLY NEVER "GET IT," BUT AT LEAST I'M TRYING!

UH...WELL, WOODY, IF YOU REALLY MEAN THAT...

WAITER! THERE'S AN ALIEN HAIR IN MY SOUP! HA, HA, HA!

48

I APPRECIATE YOUR MEETING WITH ME, MR. REDFERN.

WELL, I'M ANXIOUS TO HEAR WHAT YOU HAVE TO SAY ABOUT QUAYLE...

I SHOULD WARN YOU, THOUGH, I MAY NOT BE ABLE TO USE IT. DEA FILES CONTAIN A LOT OF RAW DATA. I'M NOT IN THE BUSINESS OF PASSING ON UNSUBSTANTIATED ALLEGATIONS.

YOU'RE RIGHT. I BETTER GO.

NO, TELL! TELL!

MR. REDFERN, PUNCHING KEYS FOR THE DEA CAN BE PRETTY TEDIOUS. SO SOMETIMES WE AMUSE OURSELVES BY "WINDOW SHOPPING"— LOOKING TO SEE IF SOME PROMINENT INDIVIDUAL HAS A FILE.

USUALLY IT'S A MICK JAGGER OR SOME FOOTBALL PLAYER. BUT LATE IN '88, AFTER QUAYLE WAS NOMINATED, SOMEONE CHECKED HIS FILE. TURNED OUT HE'D BEEN INVESTIGATED FOR PURCHASING COCAINE WHILE HE WAS A SENATOR.

WHY, THAT'S...THAT'S INCREDIBLE.

BOY, I'LL SAY.

HEY, DO YOU MIND?

ANYTHING ON MICK?

NO, MICK WAS COOL.

THE REALLY UNUSUAL THING, MR. REDFERN, WAS THAT THOSE OF US WHO ACCESSED QUAYLE'S FILE WERE DISCIPLINED. SOME OPERATORS WERE SUSPENDED, AND THE REST WERE THREATENED WITH CRIMINAL CHARGES IF WE SAID ANYTHING.

BUT SHOULDN'T YOU HAVE EXPECTED THAT?

NOT AT ALL. WE'D BEEN ACCESSING CELEBRITY FILES FOR YEARS. IT WAS ONE OF OUR PERKS. IT HAD ALWAYS BEEN WINKED AT BEFORE.

YES, BUT QUAYLE WAS DIFFERENT. ONE MORE QUAYLE BOMBSHELL COULD HAVE LOST THE ELECTION. THEY WERE DESPERATE.! THEY HAD TO SUPPRESS THE FILE AT ANY COST! BUT WHO WERE "THEY"? HOW HIGH UP DID IT GO?

THAT'S IT! THAT'S THE STORY! THE COVER-UP!

WELL, I THOUGHT SO. SHOULD I JUST PITCH THE FILE?

QUAYLE HAS A DEA FILE? DO YOU KNOW WHAT'S IN IT?

ALL I KNOW IS THAT HE WAS THE SUBJECT OF A GRAND JURY PROBE IN ONE COCAINE CASE, AND WAS MENTIONED IN CONNECTION WITH TWO OTHERS. ALL WHEN HE WAS A U.S. SENATOR.

BUT ISN'T THAT JUST HEARSAY? I MEAN, HE WASN'T INDICTED.

CORRECT. WHICH IS WHY I'M CONCENTRATING ON THE EFFORT TO COVER UP THE FILE'S EXISTENCE.

WELL, I DON'T GET IT. WHY WOULD BUSH TAKE SUCH A CHANCE NOMINATING HIM?

HE PROBABLY DIDN'T KNOW. THE FILE DIDN'T ACTUALLY SURFACE UNTIL LATE IN THE '88 CAMPAIGN.

WOW... THREE WHOLE YEARS OF DAMAGE CONTROL.

I KNOW. THEY MUST BE EXHAUSTED.

YOU KNOW, I'VE BEEN THINKING I OUGHT TO TRY TO GET IN TOUCH WITH BRETT KIMBERLIN. HE MIGHT KNOW SOMETHING ABOUT THIS...

WHO'S BRETT KIMBERLIN?

A CONVICT WHO'S SUING THE GOVERNMENT FOR TRYING TO SILENCE HIM. HE CLAIMS HE SOLD MARIJUANA TO QUAYLE ON 15 OR MORE OCCASIONS.

MARIJUANA? BUT YOU SAID QUAYLE WAS INVESTIGATED FOR BUYING COCAINE.

YEAH, BUT THE CASE WAS IN INDIANA, WHERE KIMBERLIN IS FROM. MAYBE THERE'S A CONNECTION.

I CAN'T BELIEVE WE'RE TALKING ABOUT A VICE PRESIDENT.

WELL, THEY'RE THE ONES WITH TOO MUCH TIME ON THEIR HANDS.

YOU KNOW, THE MORE I THINK ABOUT IT, THE MORE I THINK KIMBERLIN MIGHT KNOW SOMETHING ABOUT ALL THIS...

THE AUTHORITIES WENT TO AN AWFUL LOT OF TROUBLE JUST TO KEEP A CON FROM MAKING SOME MARIJUANA CHARGES THAT MOST PEOPLE WOULDN'T BELIEVE ANYWAY. SOMETHING'S VERY FISHY HERE, AND I'M GOING TO GET TO THE BOTTOM OF IT!

WILL THE PAPER PROVIDE FOR ME AND THE CHILD?

NOT SURE. I'D KEEP YOUR JOB.

HELLO? MR. KIMBERLIN? THIS IS RICK REDFERN FROM THE WASHINGTON POST...

I'M DOING A PIECE ON DAN QUAYLE FOR THE PAPER. I UNDERSTAND THAT IN PRISON YOU'VE BEEN REPEATEDLY PREVENTED FROM TALKING TO THE PRESS ABOUT QUAYLE, WHICH, FRANKLY, I DON'T GET.

IT SEEMS LIKE AN AWFUL BIG DEAL IS BEING MADE OVER A 20-YEAR-OLD MARIJUANA CLAIM. WAS THERE, BY ANY CHANCE, SOMETHING **ELSE** YOU WERE PLANNING TO REVEAL ABOUT QUAYLE HAD YOU BEEN PERMITTED TO SPEAK?

OH, YOU MEAN HIS DEA FILE?

BINGO.

MR. KIMBERLIN, WERE PRISON OFFICIALS AWARE THAT **YOU** KNEW ABOUT DAN QUAYLE'S FILE AT THE DEA?

SURE THEY WERE. THEY ROUTINELY TAPED MY PHONE CALLS. SO THEY **HAD** TO KNOW.

DO YOU THINK WORD WAS SENT BACK TO WASHINGTON?

CLIKITY CLIK! CLIK! CLIK!

I **KNOW** IT WAS. THE OFFICERS INADVERTENTLY TAPED THEIR OWN COMMENTS AS WELL AS MINE. I'VE SEEN THE TRANSCRIPT.

GOT A SAMPLE?

"HOLY COW! WAIT'LL THEY HEAR ABOUT THIS IN WASHINGTON!"

GOOD SAMPLE.

IT'S NOT JUST THE SOLITARY CONFINEMENT, MR. REDFERN. THEY'VE ALSO TRIED TO SILENCE ME BY DENYING ME PAROLE. THE SENTENCING GUIDELINES REQUIRE THAT I SERVE UP TO 92 MONTHS...

GUESS HOW LONG I'VE BEEN IN PRISON? **152** MONTHS! THAT'S AN EXTRA **FIVE YEARS!** THEY EVEN TRIED TO RECLASSIFY ME AS CATEGORY 8, WHICH IS FOR MURDERERS, SO I'D **NEVER** GET OUT!

MR. KIMBER-LIN, ARE YOU BEING MISTREATED? BY PRISON OFFICIALS?

NO, NO, NOT AT ALL. THEY KEEP CLOSE TABS ON ME, OF COURSE, BUT THEY'RE VERY NICE ABOUT IT.

UM...GUYS? SORRY TO BREAK IN, BUT I GOTTA CHANGE THE TAPE...

SEE?

MR. QUAYLE, MR. KIMBERLIN'S TREATMENT IN PRISON RAISES A HOST OF QUESTIONS. FOR INSTANCE, DID YOU PERSONALLY KNOW HE WAS PLANNING TO TELL THE PRESS ABOUT YOUR DEA FILE? DID ANYONE ELSE IN THE CAMPAIGN KNOW?

DID THE ATTORNEY GENERAL SIGN OFF ON SILENCING KIMBERLIN BY THROWING HIM INTO SOLITARY? DID YOU OR ANYONE ON YOUR STAFF COMMUNICATE WITH THE PAROLE COMMISSION? DO YOU KNOW WHY KIMBERLIN'S STILL IN PRISON?

NO, NO, NO, NO, NO AND YES.

UM... WHICH QUESTION IS THE "YES" TO?

THE ONE WHERE YOU ASK ME IF THE INTERVIEW'S OVER.

LOOK, RICK, IT'S INCREDIBLE YOU'RE EVEN **ASKING** ME ABOUT THIS! I MEAN, KIMBERLIN'S A CONVICTED DOPE DEALER! AND I'M A POLITICIAN! NOW, WHO ARE YOU GONNA BELIEVE?

I'M HERE TO TELL YOU THAT TO MY KNOWLEDGE I'VE **NEVER** USED MARIJUANA! NOR HAVE I BEEN TO A PARTY WHERE **OTHER** PEOPLE USED IT! I DON'T EVEN HAVE ANY **FRIENDS** WHO HAVE KNOWINGLY USED IT!

THAT BEING THE CASE, SIR, HOW DID YOU ARRIVE AT THE POSITION YOU TOOK AS A CONGRESSMAN THAT CONGRESS SHOULD "DEFINITELY CONSIDER" DECRIMINALIZING MARIJUANA?

UM...

YO, **THIS** I GOTTA HEAR!

AND **STAY** OUT! I'M **SICK** OF THESE PERSONAL VENDETTAS!

ZOUNDS! WHAT A SOREHEAD...

WELL, THE VEEP'S IN A TIGHT SPOT. IF KIMBERLIN'S SUIT GOES TO TRIAL, IT'LL MOST LIKELY BE SCHEDULED FOR NEXT SPRING...

THE LAST THING THE ADMINISTRATION NEEDS IS A MAJOR CIVIL SUIT DURING THE MIDDLE OF THE 1992 CAMPAIGN.

I SEE WHAT YOU MEAN.

HEY... DON'T I KNOW YOU?

GIANTS STADIUM. FALL OF '78. MEN'S ROOM.

J.J.! WHAT A SURPRISE!

HI, MA!

WHAT ARE YOU DOING HERE, HONEY?

I WAS IN THE NEIGHBORHOOD. I'VE SORT OF BEEN TOURING THE EASTERN SEABOARD.

WELL, COME ON IN. LIKE SOME HOT COCOA?

SOUNDS GOOD!

UM... HOW ABOUT YOUR PASSENGER?

NAH, LET HIM SLEEP. HE'S HAD A BAD DAY.

SO HOW HAVE YOU GUYS BEEN?

A LITTLE STRESSED OUT...

RICK'S BEEN PREPARING A MAJOR STORY ABOUT DAN QUAYLE. HE'S BEEN WORKING ON IT AROUND THE CLOCK FOR THREE WEEKS...

HE FINALLY FILED LAST NIGHT. I'M JUST GLAD HE'S WITH THE WASHINGTON POST. MOST OTHER PAPERS WOULDN'T DARE **TOUCH** A STORY LIKE THIS!

YOU **WHAT?**

KILLED IT. SORRY, RICK, WE THINK QUAYLE HAS GROWN.

... SO THEN I GOT OFF THE GARDEN STATE PARKWAY! DISASTER!

DISASTER? YOU WANT DISASTER?

THE POST JUST KILLED MY **PIECE!** IT'S "IRRESPONSIBLE"! TOO "SPECULATIVE"! I DIDN'T PROVE DRUG USE, AS IF THAT HAS **ANYTHING** TO DO WITH MY STORY!

QUAYLE'S GOT HIMSELF SOME NEW FLACKS! THE POST NOW THINKS HE'S **GROWN** IN THE JOB! HAS THE WHOLE WORLD GONE **MAD?**

HI, RICK.

HI. SOME GUY TO SEE YOU.

**HELLO?** IS MY DRIVER IN THERE?

61

AS THE RECESSION GATHERS FORCE, THE LADS BEAR DOWN.

WHY SHOULD YOU HIRE ME? BECAUSE I'M HUNGRY! I'LL GIVE 110%!

OH.

WOULD I COACH AT A HIGH SCHOOL LEVEL? IN A SECOND!

LISTEN, MAN, I DROVE AN M-1A TANK OVER 12-FOOT SAND BERMS! I THINK I CAN HANDLE A DELIVERY VAN!

POPSICLE-STICK SCULPTURES?

YEAH! PEOPLE WILL PAY A MINT FOR 'EM!

POPSICLE-STICK SCULPTURES? WHAT FOR?

TO SELL AT CRAFT FAIRS, PADRE O'MINE! AS MY CONTRIBUTION TO THE FAMILY KITTY!

I'VE ALSO SENT AWAY FOR SOME PLANT-HANGER ASSEMBLY KITS! THE MANUFACTURER PAYS YOU TO PUT 'EM TOGETHER IN THE COMFORT OF YOUR OWN HOME!

AND AS IF THAT WEREN'T ENOUGH, I'M ALSO GETTING INTO GROWING MACROBIOTIC GOURMET FOODSTUFFS!

THAT WOULD EXPLAIN THE MUSHROOMS IN YOUR BEDROOM.

NEAR THE HAMPER? NO, THOSE ARE WILD.

WHAT ARE YOU WORKING ON NOW, SON?

COTTAGE INDUSTRY NUMERO DOS, POP! MACRAME PLANT HANGERS!

WE'RE TALKING BIG BUCKS HERE! THE COMPANY PAYS $13.50 PER UNIT OF 24 ASSEMBLED HANGERS.

I CAN DO ABOUT THREE HANGERS AN HOUR. I'M NO MATH WHIZ, BUT I FIGURE IF I WORK FOUR HOURS A DAY, I SHOULD CLEAR ABOUT $3,000 A WEEK! INCREDIBLE, HUH?

I'LL SAY. GOOD LUCK.

FRANKLY, I DON'T KNOW WHY I BOTHERED WITH COLLEGE.

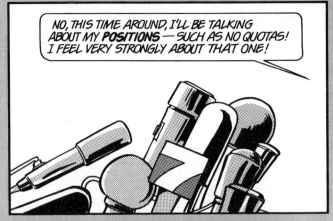

HEY, **DADS!** UP AND **AT 'EM!** GET A MOVE ON! **RISE 'N' SHINE!**

C'MON, DAD-O-RAMA! IT'S ELEVEN O'CLOCK! TIME TO GET A **MOVE ON!**

YOU'RE GOING TO BE LATE FOR YOUR JOB-SEEKERS SUPPORT GROUP! I'LL PICK OUT YOUR OUTFIT, OKAY? BE RIGHT BACK!

HOW HUMILIATING...

WHAT COLOR UNDER-PANTS DO YOU WANT?

OKAY, PEOPLE, I'M STILL JIMMY, AND THIS IS STILL THE LOWER MANHATTAN JOB-SEEKERS SUPPORT GROUP!

AS SOME OF YOU MAY HAVE HEARD, ONE OF OUR MEMBERS, ELLEN, GOT A **JOB** LAST WEEK! SHE HAD TO TAKE A BIT OF A PAY CUT, BUT SHE'S BACK TO **WORK!**

SO IT CAN BE DONE! I KNOW SOME OF YOU DON'T **FEEL** THAT WAY RIGHT NOW. I KNOW SOME OF YOU HAVE MORE OR LESS GIVEN UP...

ISN'T THAT RIGHT, MIKE?

I DUNNO. I GUESS, WHO CARES?

IT LOOKS LIKE EVERYONE'S HERE, SO WHY DON'T WE GET STARTED, OKAY, PEOPLE?

AS YOU KNOW, WE LIKE TO OPEN EVERY SESSION OF OUR JOB-SEEKERS SUPPORT GROUP WITH QUICK, PROFESSIONAL INTRODUCTIONS!

THIS LETS EVERYBODY ELSE KNOW **WHO** YOU ARE AND **WHAT** YOU ARE! MIKE, YOU LEAD OFF, AND WE'LL GO CLOCKWISE AROUND THE GROUP!

I'M MIKE. I'M A COMPLETE LOSER.

I'M HARVEY. DITTO.

WHOA, WHOA. THAT'S THE RE-CESSION SPEAKING, PEOPLE!

MIKE, LET'S WORK THROUGH THIS SELF-ESTEEM LOSS YOU'RE EXPERIENCING... TRY TO LAY OUT YOUR ASSETS, YOUR STRENGTHS. THEN WE'LL LET THE GROUP JUMP IN.

MY ASSETS? WELL, LET'S SEE. I'M A COPYWRITER. COMPETENT AT BEST. BUT HONEST ENOUGH TO WONDER WHETHER I WASN'T A FRAUD FROM THE START AND **DESERVED** TO BE FIRED.

OKAY, THAT'S MIKE'S BASELINE! WHO WANTS TO BUILD ON IT?

HE'S A SNAPPY DRESSER. NOT.

YOU KNOW, EVERYONE, MAYBE WE'RE ALL DOWN TODAY BECAUSE OF THE PAST HOLIDAY. NONE OF US COULD AFFORD MUCH CHRISTMAS THIS YEAR. MY SON ONLY GOT A BOOK, I'M ASHAMED TO SAY...

YOU THINK **THAT'S** BAD? I GAVE MY DAUGHTER A BOX OF PAPER CLIPS I STOLE FROM MY OFFICE THE DAY I WAS FIRED. THAT'S **ALL** SHE GOT!

REALLY?

YUP.

THAT **IS** PATHETIC. THANKS.

UM... I'M SURE SOMEONE HERE CAN TOP IT, RIGHT?

NO. NOPE. NOT ME.

OKAY, FOLKS, LET'S MOVE ON TO JOB OPENINGS. A FEW GREAT OPPORTUNITIES HAVE BEEN REFERRED TO ME ...

ANYONE HERE EXPERT IN INTERNATIONAL CURRENCY ISSUES? OKAY, ANYONE IN FEMTOSECOND LASERS? ANY PARALLEL COMPUTER ENGINEERS? HIV EPIDEMIOLOGISTS?

NO?... NOBODY?

OKAY, NOW, DON'T DESPAIR...

EVER FEEL YOU WERE PERFECTLY EDUCATED FOR THE BRONZE AGE?

72

Mr. John Sharp
State Comptroller
Box 13528, Capitol Station
Austin, Texas 78711

Dear Mr. Sharp:
Howdy! I'd like to become a Texan. I hereby
solemnly swear that it is my intention to
live in Texas at some later date. (I
understand there is no legal require-
ment that I actually do so, and can
change my mind later without tax penalty.)
Please send me a certificate of residency
without delay.
Sincerely,

_____
NAME

_____
MAILING ADDRESS  (BUT NOT WHERE MY HEART IS.)

_____
CITY                    STATE        ZIP

**BUSH STEPS UP TO THE TOUGH QUESTIONS..***

ANYBODY GOT A REAL CONTROVERSIAL ONE OR WANT TO MAKE A STATEMENT? I WANT SOME GUY THAT REALLY WANTS TO BE TOUGH, SOME TOUGH GUY. WHO IS IT?

*From Verbatim transcripts.*

---

**...AIDS...**

MAGIC, WHO'S ON THAT COMMISSION, FOLLOWING IN THE FOOTSTEPS OF THE EDUCATION THAT CHICK KOOP HAS PUT FORWARD TO THE BEGINNING, IS SAYING, LOOK, LIFESTYLE'S IMPORTANT.

---

**...DRUGS...**

WHERE WE'RE HURTING AS A SOCIETY IS THE 35 AND OLDER — KIND OF THE ADDICTED CROWD IS NOT SHAKING IT.

---

**...AND THE ENVIRONMENT.**

AND I LOOK OUT ON — I'LL GIVE YOU A PROBLEM OUT ON THE NORTHWEST. ALL ACROSS THE COUNTRY, WE HAVE A SPOTTED OWL PROBLEM. AND, YES, WE WANT TO SEE THAT LITTLE FURRY-FEATHERY GUY PROTECTED AND ALL OF THAT.

---

**BUSH'S WEATHER REPORT, VERBATIM.***

THE GUY OVER THERE AT PEASE — A WOMAN ACTUALLY — SHE SAID SOMETHING ABOUT A COUNTRY-WESTERN SONG ABOUT THE TRAIN, A LIGHT AT THE END OF THE TUNNEL...

*From White House transcript.*

---

I ONLY HOPE IT'S NOT A TRAIN COMING THE OTHER WAY. WELL, I SAID TO HER, WELL, I'M A COUNTRY MUSIC FAN. I LOVE IT, ALWAYS HAVE. DOESN'T FIT THE MOLD OF SOME OF THE COLUMNISTS, I MIGHT ADD, BUT NEVERTHELESS — OF WHAT THEY THINK I OUGHT TO FIT IN, BUT I LOVE IT.

---

YOU SHOULD HAVE BEEN WITH ME AT THE C.M.A. AWARDS AT NASHVILLE. BUT NEVERTHELESS, I SAID TO THEM THERE'S ANOTHER ONE THAT THE NITTY DITTY NITTY GRITTY GREAT BIRD — AND IT SAYS IF YOU WANT TO SEE A RAINBOW YOU'VE GOT TO STAND A LITTLE RAIN.

---

WE'VE HAD A LITTLE RAIN. NEW HAMPSHIRE HAS HAD TOO MUCH RAIN.

---

**BUSH ON FAITH, VERBATIM.**

AND SO I DO UNDERSTAND NEW HAMPSHIRE BECAUSE I HAVE THIS WONDERFULLY WARM FEELING THAT NEW HAMPSHIRE FEELS EXACTLY THE WAY WE DO ON THESE QUESTIONS OF FAMILY VALUES AND FAITH.

---

SOMEBODY SAID TO ME, WE PRAYED FOR YOU OVER THERE. THAT WAS NOT JUST BECAUSE I THREW UP ON THE PRIME MINISTER OF JAPAN, EITHER. WHERE WAS HE WHEN I NEEDED HIM? I SAID, LET ME TELL YOU SOMETHING.

---

AND I SAY THIS — I DON'T KNOW WHETHER ANY MINISTERS FROM THE EPISCOPAL CHURCH ARE HERE — I HOPE SO. BUT I SAID TO HIM THIS: YOU'RE ON TO SOMETHING HERE. YOU CANNOT BE PRESIDENT OF THE UNITED STATES IF YOU DON'T HAVE FAITH.

---

IT'S BEEN GREAT. I'LL GO BACK TO WASHINGTON ALL FIRED UP FOR TOMORROW AND TACKLE THE PRESIDENT OR THE PRIME MINISTER OF THIS OR THE GOVERNOR OF THAT COMING IN. BUT I'LL HAVE THIS HEARTBEAT...

82

CANDIDATE DUKE IS STEAMED.

YOU SEE HOW THEY *TWISTED* MY WORDS ABOUT THE KLAN? I *TOLD* YOU THAT INTERVIEW WAS A BAD IDEA!

LOOK, CUZ, IT GOT YOU INK, DIDN'T IT? IT MOVED ON THE WIRES, GOT YOUR NAME OUT THERE AGAIN!

ONCE AGAIN, THE MEDIA PLAYED RIGHT INTO YOUR HANDS! DESPITE THE BEST EFFORTS OF YOUR CRITICS...

...YOU'VE GROWN IN STATURE!

REALLY? YOU NOTICE A DIFFERENCE?

WHAT I DON'T UNDERSTAND IS WHY I KEEP GETTING REAMED BY THE MEDIA, WHILE PAT BUCHANAN, WHO'S *JUST* AS CONSERVATIVE, GETS A FREE RIDE!

YOU'RE RIGHT, DAVEY BOY, IT STINKS...

LISTEN TO SOME OF WHAT HE'S GOTTEN AWAY WITH! HE CALLED HITLER "AN INDIVIDUAL OF GREAT COURAGE... EXTRAORDINARY GIFTS."

WHAT? *BUCHANAN* SAID THAT? WHY, THAT'S... THAT'S... *OUTRAGEOUS!*

TELL ME ABOUT IT.

HITLER'S *MY* FRANCHISE, DAMMIT!

I SAY CALL HIM ON IT. LET HIM FIND HIS OWN BOYHOOD HEROES.

YOU'RE RIGHT, CUZ! IT'S *BUCHANAN* WE'VE GOT TO KEEP AN EYE ON, NOT THAT GOOFBALL IN THE ROSE GARDEN!

BUCHANAN'S EVEN MOVING IN ON YOUR IMMIGRATION ISSUE! HE'S NOW ADVOCATING THE "BUCHANAN FENCE," A 1500-MILE TRENCH TO KEEP OUT THE WETBACKS!

OH, RIGHT! AND WHO'S SUPPOSED TO PAY FOR IT? AND WHO'S GOING TO MAN IT? WILL THEY SHOOT TO KILL? WILL THERE BE DOGS? AND WHO'S GOING TO BE RESPONSIBLE FOR RETRIEVING THE BODIES?

HE HASN'T SAID...

EXACTLY! WEAK ON SPECIFICS!

THAT'S WHAT I'VE BEEN SAYING. A SLICK PROPOSAL, BUT WHERE'S THE *BEEF?*

THERE'S NO WAY AROUND IT—WE'VE GOT TO TAKE THE OFFENSIVE AGAINST BUCHANAN!

HOW WE GOING TO DO THAT?

THE SAME WAY THEY'VE BEEN NAILING ME—INNUENDO ABOUT THE PAST!

THINK ABOUT IT, MAN—WHAT'S THE **ONLY** THING WORSE THAN HAVING BEEN A LONG-TIME MEMBER OF THE KU KLUX KLAN?

MR. BUCHANAN, HOW DO YOU EX-PLAIN YOUR 17 YEARS IN THE MEDIA?

YOUTHFUL INDISCRE-TION.

PAT BUCHANAN, UNDER FIRE.

MR. BUCHANAN, HOW DO YOU RESPOND TO CHARGES FROM DAVID DUKE THAT YOU'RE A FORMER MEMBER OF THE NATIONAL MEDIA?

THAT'S A VICIOUS SMEAR AND IT COMES FROM A LIT-TLE GUTTERSNIPE SO TWO-FACED HE HAD TO HIDE ONE OF THEM UNDER A SHEET AND HAVE THE OTHER ONE CHEMICALLY PEELED!

UM...IS THAT A DENIAL?

HEY, GUY, IF I **HAD** BEEN A MEMBER OF THE MEDIA, WOULD I TELL **YOU**?

BUT THERE'S... THERE'S VIDEOTAPE!

OKAY, SO I EXPERIMENTED WITH CABLE. I DIDN'T LIKE IT.

©B Trudeau

LET ME GET THIS STRAIGHT, MR. BUCHANAN. YOU'RE SAYING YOU ONLY **EXPERI-MENTED** WITH JOURNALISM?

YES. I TRIED IT A FEW TIMES, BUT I DIDN'T LIKE IT.

THE FACT IS, THIS IS **OLD NEWS!** IT'S BEEN CHECKED OUT A **MILLION** TIMES WITH MY FORMER "COLLEAGUES"!

OF ALL THE PEOPLE I'M ALLEGED TO HAVE WORKED WITH—MY SYNDICATE EDITOR, MY PRODUCER AT CNN, MY PARTNER ON **"CROSSFIRE"**—NOT **ONE** OF THEM HAS EVER ACCUSED ME OF BEING A PROFESSIONAL JOURNALIST!

©B Trudeau

IT'S TRUE—THAT PART CHECKS OUT.

DON'T BELIEVE ME? FOLLOW ME AROUND! TRY TO CATCH ME PUTTING SOMETHING TO BED!

BOYS! GIRLS! TIRED OF LOSING SINGING ENGAGEMENTS BECAUSE OF RUMORS LINKING **YOU** TO A PRESIDENTIAL CANDIDATE? SICK OF ALL THE LIES AND DECEIT?

WELL, NOW YOU CAN COME FORWARD — **WITHOUT** HAVING TO TALK TO SOME SWEATY, OVERWEIGHT TABLOID REPORTER! YES, THIS SYNDICATED FAMILY FEATURE IS INTERESTED IN **YOUR** STORY!

NOW, I KNOW WHAT YOU'RE THINKING — "HAVEN'T WE HAD ENOUGH SLEAZE FOR ONE CAMPAIGN?" WELL, LET ME PUT IT THIS WAY...

HOW DOES $25 SOUND?

*TOMORROW: AN EXCITING CASH OFFER!*

THAT'S RIGHT, KIDS, YOU HEARD CORRECTLY! IF YOU'VE SLEPT WITH ANY CURRENT PRESIDENTIAL CANDIDATE, THIS FEATURE WILL PAY YOU $25 TO TELL **YOUR** STORY!

OH, SURE, YOU COULD ALWAYS SELL IT TO THE TABS FOR MORE, BUT WOULDN'T YOU RATHER SEE A DIGNIFIED RE-ENACTMENT OF YOUR STORY BY NATIONALLY KNOWN CARTOON PERSONALITIES? CHECK OUT THIS PILOT PANEL!

"OH. OH. OH. OH. OH. OH."

"WELL, GOTTA RUN."

YES, THAT COULD BE **YOUR** STORY! ACT NOW!

*TOMORROW: Complete entry forms!*

THAT'S RIGHT, CAMPERS. IF YOU'VE EVER SLEPT WITH A PRESIDENTIAL HOPEFUL — OR KNOW SOMEONE **ELSE** WHO HAS — WE WANT TO GIVE YOU $25 IN **COLD, HARD CASH!**

TO FIND OUT IF YOUR STORY IS PRURIENT ENOUGH TO QUALIFY, JUST FILL OUT THE ATTACHED "**TRASH-FOR-CASH**" ENTRY FORM AND SEND IT TO ME, CARE OF THIS PAPER! **GOOD LUCK!**

### CAMPAIGN '92 — TRASH-FOR-CASH

**1. I have trash on:** (CHECK ONE)
- [ ] Bill Clinton
- [ ] Paul Tsongas
- [ ] Jerry Brown
- [ ] Tom Harkin
- [ ] Bob Kerrey
- [ ] George Bush

**2. My story involves:**
- [ ] me
- [ ] my best friend
- [ ] my evil twin
- [ ] my publicist
- [ ] a Republican operative
- [ ] Geraldo

**3. I would describe my relationship with the candidate as:**
- [ ] torrid, steamy
- [ ] a defining moment
- [ ] the right thing to do
- [ ] videotaped
- [ ] in litigation

**4. The candidate used to call me:**
- [ ] "Babe"
- [ ] "Mommy"
- [ ] "Commissioner"
- [ ] from convenience store pay phones

*TO BE CONTINUED...*

OKAY, BOYS AND GIRLS, HERE'S PART TWO OF OUR CAMPAIGN '92 "TRASH-FOR-CASH" ENTRY BLANK! FILL IT IN AND SEND IT TO ME, CARE OF THIS PAPER! / IF WE USE YOUR STORY, WE'LL SEND YOU 25 BIG ONES!

## CAMPAIGN '92 — TRASH-FOR-CASH

**5. My relationship with the candidate lasted:**
- ☐ 12 years
- ☐ 60 days
- ☐ 60 seconds
- ☐ Not sure

**6. The last thing that the candidate said to me was:**
- ☐ "This will not stand."
- ☐ "Need a job?"
- ☐ "Cuomo's acting like an Italian-American stereotype."
- ☐ "Message: I care."
- ☐ "What's that whirring sound?"

**7. I believe my story will:**
- ☐ restore my good name
- ☐ help me find a husband
- ☐ make my parents proud
- ☐ get me a record deal
- ☐ benefit mankind

**8. My name is:**
- ☐ Gennifer with a "G"
- ☐ Jennifer with a "J"
- ☐ Kandy with a "K"
- ☐ Carrii with two "i's"
- ☐ Karee with a "K", one "r" and two "e's"
- ☐ Other _____

CLIP 'N' SEND **TODAY!** ACT NOW, AND YOU'LL BE ELIGIBLE FOR A **FREE SCREEN TEST!**

OKAY, NOW FOR THE TOUGH PART, GANG — THE ESSAY QUESTIONS! PLEASE READ SILENTLY / WHILE I READ ALOUD...

## CAMPAIGN '92 — TRASH-FOR-CASH

**9.** You're dating a married father of three with presidential ambitions. You believe that you and he have a future together. Explain.

**10. Name three movies** *besides* **"Pretty Woman"** that have helped shape your personal philosophy.

YOU MAY NOW **BEGIN!** REMINDER TO ALL YOU GENNIFERS: SPELLING COUNTS!

SOME OF YOU MAY BE WONDERING WHY WE'VE INCLUDED THE BUSH-MEISTER IN OUR "TRASH-FOR-CASH" OFFER...

WHY? SIMPLE **FAIRNESS!** WHY SHOULD THE PUTATIVE G.O.P. NOMINEE NOT BE HELD TO THE SAME STANDARDS OF PERSONAL CONDUCT THAT HIS COMPETITION IS?

TRUE, TRASHING THE REPUTATION OF A SITTING PRESIDENT FOR $25 DOES SEEM A BIT BEYOND THE PALE. BUT TO THOSE WHO WOULD DEMUR, LET ME ASK THIS...

HOW'S **ANOTHER** 25 SMACKS SOUND? HUH? **HUH?**

HELLO? I'M SICK OF THE LIES...

GREETINGS FROM NEW HAMPSHIRE! I'M ROLAND HEDLEY, AND THIS IS A SPECIAL EDITION OF "ROLLIE'S PICKS", MY QUADRENNIAL CAMPAIGN FORECAST!

BECAUSE OF THE LONG LEAD TIME REQUIRED TO PROCESS THIS EXQUISITELY HAND-COLORED SUNDAY FEATURE, I'M ACTUALLY SPEAKING TO YOU FROM THE VANTAGE OF JANUARY 10, OVER **TWO MONTHS** AGO...

...WHICH MAKES MY PRESIDENTIAL PROGNOSTICATIONS ALL THE **BOLDER!** UNLIKE MOST PUNDITS, I CAN'T REVISE MY PROJECTIONS! I'M LOCKED IN, WORKING WITHOUT A NET, PUTTING MY REPUTATION **ON THE LINE!**

OKAY, LET'S GET TO IT! ON THE DEMOCRATIC SIDE, IT'S **JERRY BROWN** BREAKING OUT OF THE PACK, WITH **TOM HARKIN** CLOSE BEHIND! **TSONGAS** IS DEAD, AND **CLINTON**, WHOSE RUMORED AFFAIRS NEVER SURFACED, HAS BEEN MORTALLY WOUNDED BY LACK OF PRESS COVERAGE!

ON THE G.O.P. SIDE, **BUSH** HAS BEEN BATTERED BY UNSUBSTANTIATED ALLEGATIONS OF INFIDELITY, LEAVING THE FIELD WIDE OPEN FOR **DAVID DUKE**, WHO HAS MADE SHORT WORK OF FELLOW FRUITCAKE **PAT BUCHANAN!**

GB Trudeau

THERE YOU HAVE IT— MY **PRE-SEASON** PICKS AS NOTARIZED BELOW! AM I ON THE MONEY? **YOU** BE THE JUDGE!

NOTARIZED ON THIS DAY
January 10, 1992
BY Alan J. Weil
ALAN J. WEIL, C.P.A.

YOU KNOW, POP, IT'S STILL HARD TO THINK ABOUT THOSE WHO HAD TO SERVE IN VIETNAM AND THOSE WHO DIDN'T...

YOU REMEMBER SPARKY WALLER, MY BEST FRIEND IN HIGH SCHOOL? WE HAD ABOUT THE SAME GRADES, BUT SPARKY COULDN'T AFFORD COLLEGE, SO THEY NAILED HIM.

THE GUY WAS ON HIS WAY TO VIETNAM WITHIN SIX MONTHS. HE WAS ASSIGNED TO A MOTOR POOL, AND HE SPENT THE WHOLE WAR SITTING AROUND COMPLETELY STONED, LISTENING TO ROCK MUSIC.

THAT COULD HAVE BEEN **ME**, DAD!

THAT **WAS** YOU, SON.

©B Trudeau

I'LL NEVER FORGET THE NIGHT OF THE LOTTERY, DAD. A FRIEND TOLD ME I WAS NUMBER 27...

I WAS DEVASTATED. I THOUGHT I'D BEEN HANDED A DEATH SENTENCE. I WENT BACK TO MY ROOM, TURNED OUT THE LIGHTS, AND JUST STARED OUT THE WINDOW AT THE CITY...

AS A LIGHT SNOW BEGAN TO FALL, TWO YOUNG REVELERS TUMBLED OUT OF A BAR INTO THE STREET, LAUGHING AND SHOUTING WITH JOY. IN ONE NIGHT, IT SEEMED, AN ENTIRE GENERATION HAD BEEN NEATLY DIVIDED INTO WINNERS AND LOSERS!

WOW... THAT'S A POWERFUL IMAGE, SON.

YEAH. TURNED OUT THEY WERE JUST A COUPLE OF DANISH SAILORS, BUT IT STAYED WITH ME.

©B Trudeau

94